Divers
of the
Deep Sea

Marianne Morrison

Contents

CHAPTER 1

The Oceans

People have explored Earth for as long as people have been on Earth. We know a lot about Earth. We have been to the highest mountain. We have explored the deepest forests. We have traveled to the North and South Poles. But if you think we have explored most of Earth, think again.

Do you think of Earth as a water planet? You might be surprised to find out that most of Earth is covered by water. In fact, the Earth is covered by about three times more water than land.

Look at the map below. The blue shows where the oceans are. That's a lot of water! And most of it has never been explored.

The Ocean Depths

Explorers have traveled across the ocean for centuries. We know a lot about the surface, or top, of the ocean. But what lies below the surface?

dolphin

bluefin tuna

great white shark

jellyfish

sperm whale

giant squid

anglerfish

flapjack devilfish

whale fish

deepwater jelly fish

tripod fish

sea spider

sea cucumber

Note: Creatures and zones are not drawn to scale.

The ocean is divided into four zones. The amount of light and the **depth** of the water change from zone to zone.

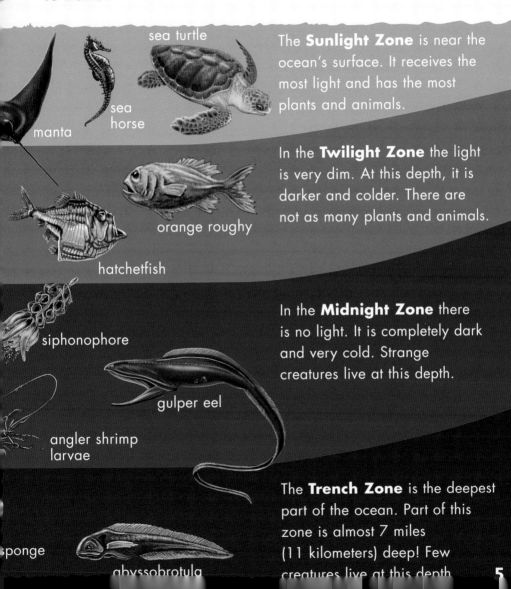

sea turtle

sea horse

manta

The **Sunlight Zone** is near the ocean's surface. It receives the most light and has the most plants and animals.

orange roughy

hatchetfish

In the **Twilight Zone** the light is very dim. At this depth, it is darker and colder. There are not as many plants and animals.

siphonophore

gulper eel

angler shrimp larvae

In the **Midnight Zone** there is no light. It is completely dark and very cold. Strange creatures live at this depth.

sponge

abyssobrotula

The **Trench Zone** is the deepest part of the ocean. Part of this zone is almost 7 miles (11 kilometers) deep! Few creatures live at this depth.

CHAPTER 2

Divers Go Deeper

The Diving Helmet

People have always wanted to explore below the surface of the ocean. The earliest divers held their breath and went as deep as they could go before needing more air. That wasn't very deep.

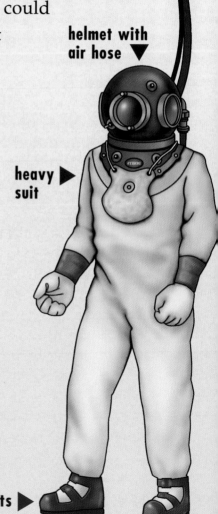

helmet with air hose ▼

Then the **diving helmet** was invented in 1839. It was copper and very heavy. The helmet was attached to a heavy diving suit. An air hose from the helmet to the surface brought air to the diver. Heavy boots with lead weights helped the diver sink to the bottom and stay down. Divers could go down and walk around 230 feet (70 meters) below the surface.

heavy ▶ suit

boots with lead weights ▶

Eyewitness Report

Place: Aegean Sea, off the coast of Greece
Date: May 1869

It takes 30 minutes for the diver to put on his diving gear. The heavy helmet is finally bolted to his suit. The air hose is attached. Weights are put on his chest and his back. His boots also have lead weights on the bottoms.

Finally, he is helped into the water. The weights help him sink. Air pumps into his helmet as he goes down.

He looks through the faceplate in his helmet. A parrotfish swims up to get a better look at him. A school of squid seems to hang in the water.

Finally, he is 230 feet (70 meters) below the surface. A ray rises from the sandy bottom. The diver starts to walk slowly towards the rocky ledge where sponges grow. He begins to collect the sponges that he will sell.

The Aqua-Lung

Divers could go deeper with the diving helmet, but they still wanted to move around freely. They dreamed of swimming like fish. In 1943, Jacques Cousteau made this dream come true. He invented the **Aqua-Lung**. This tank allowed the diver to breathe air and move about freely underwater. It was the start of scuba diving.

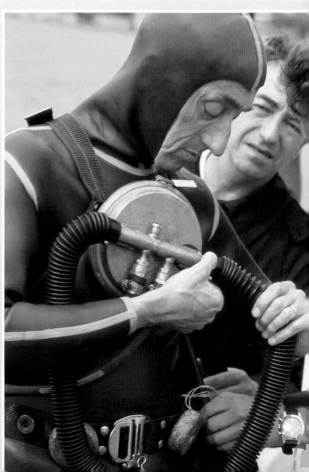

Jacques Cousteau ▶
prepares to dive.
Divers have gone as deep
as 210 feet (64 meters)
using the Aqua-Lung.

Eyewitness Report

Diver: **Jacques Cousteau**
Place: **Mediterranean Sea, off the coast of France**
Date: **June 1943**

Cousteau straps the heavy tanks of air on his back. He puts on his diving mask. He puts on his diving fins. With 50 pounds (23 kilograms) on his back, he waddles into the sea.

He looks down and sees a canyon far below. He kicks his fins and starts down. He glides through the water like a fish. Then he lets the air out of his lungs. He watches the bubbles rise. Next he takes a deep breath. It works! He can breathe underwater.

Cousteau's dream has come true. He can swim freely. There are no ropes, hoses, or a heavy helmet to slow him down. He rolls over. He does a somersault. He even stands upside down on one finger.

The Jim Suit

Divers wanted to go much deeper and still be able to move around freely. This was a problem. The deeper you go the colder it gets. You start to feel as if you are being crushed because of **water pressure**. Water pressure is the weight of water. The more water above you, the more weight presses on you.

The **Jim suit** was invented to let divers roam freely in very deep water. It is named for the first man who used it, Jim Jarratt. The Jim suit is a heavy metal suit. It looks like a spacesuit. It protects the diver from the cold and the water pressure.

Attached to the arms are two metal claws for lifting things. Inside, the diver can breathe air that is cleaned and then **recycled**. For most dives in the Jim suit, the diver is lowered on a rope from the surface.

Sylvia Earle dove 1,250 feet ▶ (381 meters) in a Jim suit strapped to a small submarine.

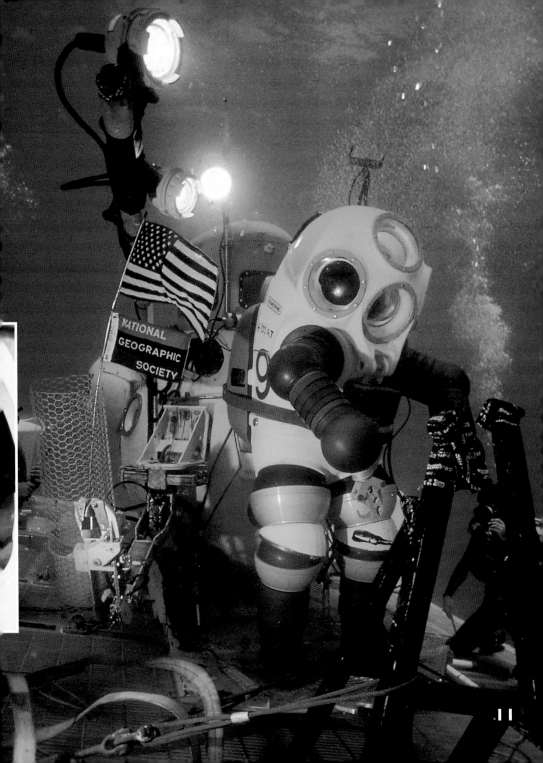

Eyewitness Report

Diver: Sylvia Earle
Place: Pacific Ocean, off the coast of Hawaii
Date: October 19, 1979

Everything around her is blue as she begins her dive. Earle is strapped to a small submarine. As she goes deeper, the water changes from blue to gray and finally black. She feels a soft thump as the submarine touches the bottom.

Finally, they stop at 1,250 feet (381 meters). The pilot releases the strap holding her onto the submarine. She is free to explore the deep.

A small circle of light from the sub shows an amazing and wonderful world. A dozen bright red crabs with long legs sway on a red sea fan. A lantern fish swims by with lights glowing on its side. Earle looks away from the light and sees sparks of living light. Tiny fish light up as they brush against her. She explores strange coral that glows in the dark.

After two and a half hours on the ocean floor, Earle heads back to the surface.

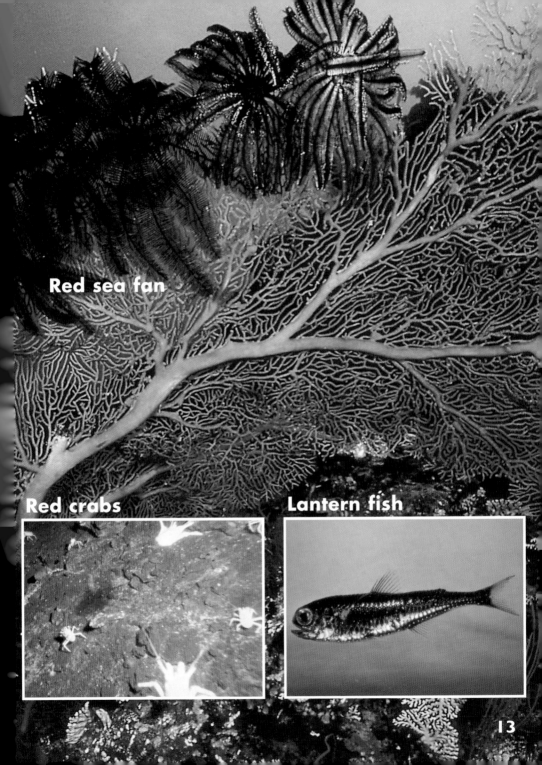

Red sea fan

Red crabs

Lantern fish

13

CHAPTER 3

Diving Ships Go Deeper

The Bathysphere

Parts of the ocean are almost 7 miles (11 kilometers) deep. People wanted to go there, but they needed to invent diving ships that would take them deep enough. To make these deep dives possible, William Beebe and Otis Barton invented the **bathysphere**.

This strange round chamber on a wire cable was like an elevator to the deep. It could go up and down but it couldn't move sideways. The bathysphere looked like a giant eye. The divers inside recorded every animal that passed before its round window, or porthole.

William Beebe and Otis ▲ Barton dove 3,028 feet (924 meters) in the bathysphere.

Beebe and Barton were the first to enter that zone of the ocean where there is no light at all. Only the light from a small bulb inside the bathysphere helped them see the amazing things of the Midnight Zone.

Eyewitness Report

Divers: **William Beebe and Otis Barton**
Place: **Atlantic Ocean, off the coast of Bermuda**
Date: **August 15, 1934**

Beebe squeezes head first through the small opening to get inside. Once inside he makes room for Barton. There's not much room. They untangle their legs and get ready. Then the heavy door is bolted shut.

They begin to go down. The deeper they go, the darker it gets. It also gets colder, much colder. Then they start to see the strange creatures of the deep. An anglerfish swims by. As they go deeper, several hatchetfish swim through the beam of light from their little light bulb.

Finally, they enter the Midnight Zone of the ocean. This is a world of complete and total darkness. They reach a depth of 3,028 feet (924 meters). They stay there for only three minutes. They have just enough air for the trip to the surface.

Anglerfish

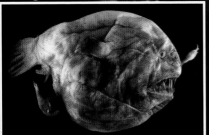

Hatchetfish

The Bathyscaph

To help divers go even deeper, a diving ship was invented. This ship was called a **bathyscaph**. It could move up and down but could not move around easily.

In 1960, Jacques Piccard and Don Walsh used a bathyscaph named the *Trieste* to dive almost 7 miles (11 kilometers) down. They explored the Trench Zone, the deepest known part of the ocean.

No person has ever returned to this depth. These two men still hold the record for the deepest dive.

Jacques Piccard and Don Walsh dove to the bottom of the ocean in the *Trieste*.

Eyewitness Report

Divers: **Jacques Piccard and Don Walsh**
Place: **Pacific Ocean, off the coast of Guam**
Date: **January 23, 1960**

Huge waves pound the *Trieste* as Piccard and Walsh climb on board. Then, at 8:23 in the morning, they begin their dive.

Three hours later they are 27,000 feet (8,235 meters) deep and still going down. They go deeper and deeper.

As they near the bottom, fear comes over them. What if the ocean bottom is a thick ooze? The ship could get stuck. No one could save them. They would freeze to death in this cold, black world.

Finally, they reach the bottom. They do not get stuck. They are 35,800 feet (10,919 meters) deep. This is almost 7 miles (11 kilometers) down. Piccard looks out. He sees a flatfish with two round eyes swimming away. Life exists this deep!

They spend only 20 minutes on the bottom before they begin to go up. After more than eight and half hours, the dive is over. They reach the surface again.

Submersibles

A **submersible** is like a small submarine. Once in the water, a submersible can move around. It also has lights that help divers see underwater. An explorer can stay underwater in it for about ten hours.

Today, divers use many different machines to explore the deep. Some submersibles have robots attached to them. The crew inside the submersible can send the robot into small places. A camera on the robot sends pictures back.

In 1986, Robert Ballard led a team to explore the *Titanic*. This famous ship sank in 1912 and was over 2 miles (3 kilometers) deep when found. Ballard went down in the submersible named *Alvin*. Attached to *Alvin* was the robot named *Jason Junior*, or *JJ*.

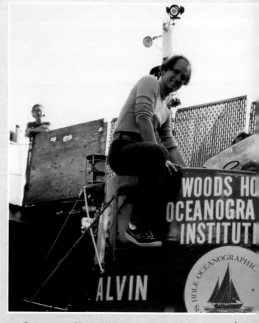

Robert Ballard dove 12,460 feet ▶ (3,800 meters) in *Alvin* to explore the *Titanic*.

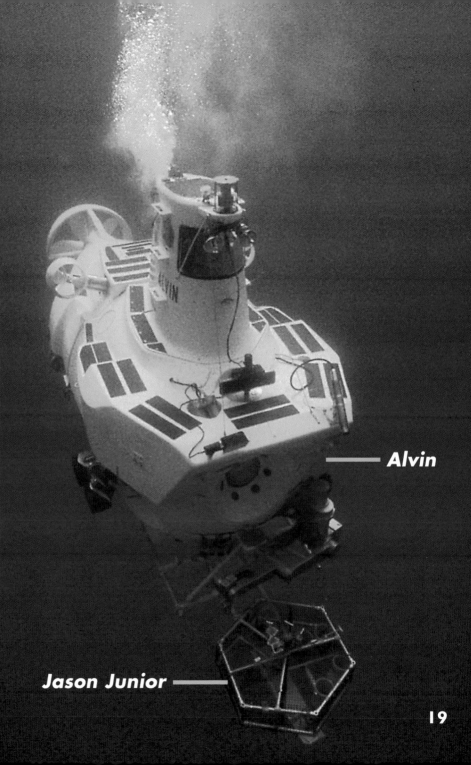

Alvin

Jason Junior

19

Eyewitness Report

Diver: **Robert Ballard**
Place: **Atlantic Ocean, off the coast of Newfoundland**
Date: **July 1986**

It takes more than two hours to get down to the *Titanic*. This is the third dive to the *Titanic* in the little submersible *Alvin*. But this is the first time Ballard and his team will use the robot *JJ* to explore the inside of the ship.

They reach the deck of the ship. Slowly they steer *Alvin* inside. They go down the main staircase of the ship. Then they park *Alvin* and send *JJ* out into the ship. They guide the robot down into the ship. They see the grand clock on the landing of the staircase. Then they see a beautiful light hanging from the ceiling by its cord.

The team makes ten more dives after this one. They see an amazing collection of things from the ship. They see the dinner plates, beds, sinks, bathtubs, doorknobs, and windows that were once part of this great ship. They are the first explorers to find and explore this famous sunken ship.

JJ at a window of the *Titanic*

Dinner plates on the *Titanic*

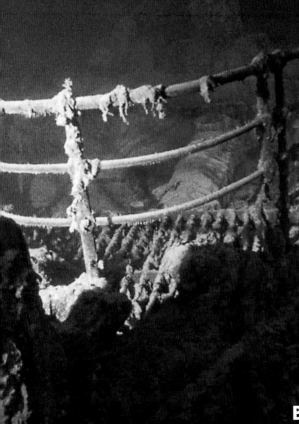

Bow of the *Titanic*

A History of Deep Sea Dives

1. **Diving Helmet:**
   230 feet (70 meters).
   Augustus Siebe invented the
   closed diving helmet in 1839.

2. **Aqua-Lung: 210 feet**
   (64 meters). Jacques Cousteau
   makes the first dive with
   an Aqua-Lung in 1943.

3. **Jim Suit: 1,250 feet**
   (381 meters). Sylvia Earle
   completes the deepest solo
   dive in Jim suit in 1979.

4. **Bathysphere: 3,028 feet**
   (924 meters). William Beebe
   and Otis Barton reach the
   Midnight Zone in 1934.

5. **Submersible: 12,460 feet**
   (3,800 meters). Robert Ballard
   explores the *Titanic* using
   Alvin in 1986.

6. **Bathyscaph: 35,800 feet**
   (10,919 meters). Jacques Piccard
   and Don Walsh reach ocean
   bottom in 1960.

Glossary

Aqua-Lung   an underwater breathing machine that enables a diver to swim freely

bathyscaph   a diving ship designed for deep-sea exploration

bathysphere   a round diving ship that could only go straight up and down

depth   how deep something is in the water

diving helmet   copper helmet with an air hose that brings fresh air from the surface to the diver

Jim suit   self-contained, deep water diving suit for a single diver

recycled   to be reused

submersible   a small underwater craft used for deep-sea research

water pressure   the weight of water

Index